Start with Art

Sports and Leisure

© Aladdin Books Ltd 2000

Designed and produced by
Aladdin Books Ltd
28 Percy Street
London W1P 0LD

ISBN 0-7613-1210-2 (lib. bdg.)
0-7613-0844-X (pbk.)

First published in the United States
in 2000 by
Copper Beech Books,
an imprint of
The Millbrook Press
2 Old New Milford Road
Brookfield, Connecticut 06804

Project Editor
Sally Hewitt

Editor
Liz White

Designer
Flick Killerby

Illustrator
Catherine Ward—SGA

Picture Research
Brooks Krikler Research

Printed in Belgium
All rights reserved

Original Design Concept
David West Children's Books

Cataloging-in-Publication data is on file at the Library of Congress

The project editor, Sally Hewitt, is an experienced teacher. She writes and
edits books for children on a wide variety of subjects including art, music,
science, and math.

The author, Sue Lacey, is an experienced teacher of art. She currently
teaches primary schoolchildren in the south of England. In her spare time,
she paints and sculpts.

photocredits: Abbreviations: t-top, m-middle, b-bottom, r-right, l-left, c-center
Pages 4, 7, 11, 13, 15, 16, 19, 20, 23, 27, & 29 - AKG London. 24—The Musée Picasso, Paris © Succession
Picasso / DACS 2000. 30 AKG©Salvador Dali—Foundation Gala-Salvador Dali / DACS 2000.

Start *with* Art

Sports and Leisure

Sue Lacey

COPPER BEECH BOOKS
BROOKFIELD • CONNECTICUT

INTRODUCTION

Artists work with many different tools and materials to make art. They also spend a great deal of time looking carefully at patterns, shapes, and colors.

This book is about how artists see **sports and leisure**. In the past, before television, computers, and movies, people had very different ways of spending their leisure time. They would go on picnics, sit in cafés, or perhaps go on boat trips. You can see this in their paintings.

You don't have to be a brilliant artist to do the projects in this book. Just have fun being creative.

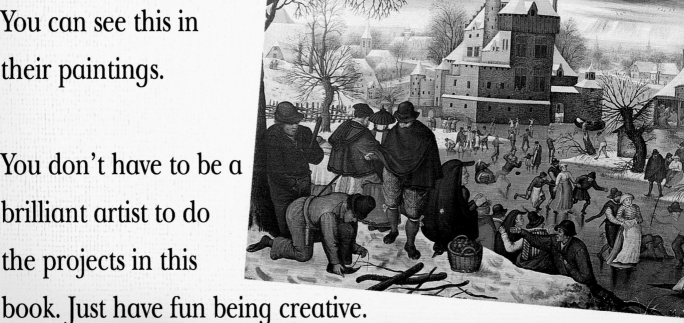

CONTENTS

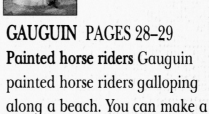

WORKING LIKE AN ARTIST

It can help you in your work if you start by looking carefully and collecting ideas, just like an artist. Artists usually carry a sketchbook around with them all the time so they can get their ideas on paper right away.

Words
You can write some words to remind you of the shapes, colors, and patterns you see.

Materials
Try out different pencils, pens, paints, pastels, crayons, and materials to see what they do. Which would be the best for this work?

Color
When using color, mix all the colors you want first and try them out. It is amazing how many different colors you can make.

Using a sketchbook Before you start each project, this is the place to do your sketches. Try out your tools and materials, mix colors, and stick in some interesting papers and fabrics. You can then choose which you want to use.

Be a magpie

Make a collection of things that are of interest to you like feathers, stones, or materials. Anything that catches your eye could be useful in your artwork.

Art box You can collect tools and materials together for your work and put them in a box. Sometimes you may need to go to an art store to buy exactly what you need. Often you can find things at home you can use. Ask for something for your art box for your birthday!

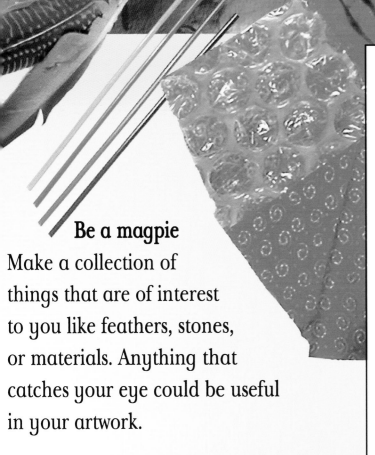

Drawing sporting figures

It can seem difficult to draw people in action, but if you take your time, make some sketches, and look carefully, you can do it!

Body shapes

Start by drawing simple shapes to show the head, arms, and legs. Look at how the body is made up.

Try to break the body down into easy lines. Think of the shoulders as one line, the arms and legs as others.

Make sure you have made the head the right size, and check that the legs are not too long or too short.

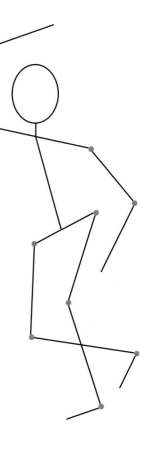

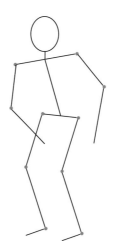

Look at where the joints are and how they move.

Once you have mastered this and the proportions look right, try drawing a different pose using the same technique.

WHAT YOU NEED
Thick white paper
India ink
Water
Sketchbook
Paintbrush

USING INKS

By adding different amounts of water to one color, August Macke could paint using different shades of blue. Why not try using inks to paint a picnic picture? Add different amounts of water to the color you choose to make different tones.

PROJECT: PAINTING WITH INK

Step 1. Make a sketch of a picnic scene on thick white paper. In your sketchbook, mix some india ink with water to make three tones of the same color—dark, medium, and light.

Step 2. Starting with the light tone, paint in the shapes. While the ink is still wet, paint in the medium and dark tones.

GALLERY

The Picnic After Sailing 1913
AUGUST MACKE (1887–1914)

WATERCOLORS
Macke usually painted in bright oil paint, but he was also skilled with watercolors.

PICNIC
Many artists at this time painted picnic scenes.

SHADES
How many different shades of blue can you see in this painting?

COLOR
The boat tells us that this was a river picnic and could be the reason Macke chose watery colors.

Although the German artist August Macke was a good student, he left school to become a painter before taking his final exams. He soon met other famous artists who decided to paint using colors full of feeling. When he died in 1914, during World War I, his friend Marc said, "With the loss of his harmony of colors, German art will become paler."

EXPRESSIONIST BOAT TRIP

WHAT YOU NEED
Selection of paper
and cardboard
Fabrics • Pencil
Paper • Scissors
Glue

The colors and shapes used by Gabriele Münter are very pleasing to the eye and can easily be turned into a collage. If you draw, cut, and paste together some simple shapes cut from cardboard or fabrics, you can make a boating scene of your own.

PROJECT: BOATING COLLAGE

Step 1. Draw your picture of a boating scene onto cardboard using simple shapes. Collect different papers and fabrics that are good colors for your scene.

Step 2. Cut out mountains, fields, and water shapes for the background and water. Arrange them on the cardboard. Add a boat and people.

Step 3. When you are happy with the arrangement, glue everything in place.

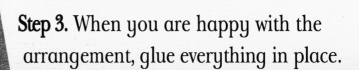

GALLERY

Boat Trip 1910
GABRIELE MÜNTER (1877–1962)

PEOPLE
A group of Expressionist artists used to go on vacation together each year to paint. Could this be the artists on a boat trip?

SHAPE
Münter liked to change what she saw into simpler shapes and colors.

COMPOSITION
The arrangement of people, background, colors, and shapes cleverly draws your eye around the picture.

FEELING
How does this picture make you feel? Do you think Münter liked boat trips?

When Gabriele Münter started painting in Germany, women were not allowed to put their pictures into art exhibitions with men. They were expected to stay at home and look after their families. But Gabriele spent her life painting. She particularly liked painting people. She said her work was about "self-expression," and she became a member of the Expressionist group of painters.

ANCIENT GREEK ART

Pottery in ancient Greek times was made by specially trained potters who were very skilled in using clay. Pots and bowls can be made out of papier-mâché, too, so follow the instructions and try it for yourself!

WHAT YOU NEED
Glass or plastic kitchen bowl
Plastic wrap • Paints
Newspaper • Flour
Water • Paintbrush
Glue • Cardboard
Scissors

PROJECT: PAPIER-MÂCHÉ BOWL

Step 1. Ask if you may use a glass or plastic kitchen bowl, and line it with plastic wrap.

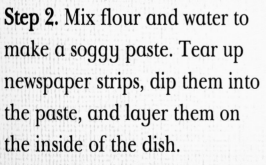

Step 2. Mix flour and water to make a soggy paste. Tear up newspaper strips, dip them into the paste, and layer them on the inside of the dish.

Step 3. Make five or six layers, leaving the papier-mâché to dry between layers. When it is all dry, lift the paper bowl out carefully. You could add handles.

Step 4. Paint your bowl black or bl[...] on the outside and terra-cotta red [...] inside. Cut out some athletes from orange cardboard or paper and paste them around the pot.

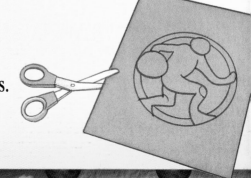

GALLERY

Greek Red-Figure Vase c510/500 B.C.
ANCIENT GREECE

OLYMPICS
Greek men and women enjoyed athletics and held the first Olympic Games. Many vases showed athletes taking part in games.

BACKGROUND
The black background of the pot was painted with a special clay that turned black when heated.

USE
What do you think this vase was used for?

This is a picture from a vase made by a Greek potter long ago. Potters would make a vase or bowl out of red clay. They would then paint the pottery with liquid clay and draw figures on the surface using a sharp tool. The heat of the kiln turned the liquid clay black, and the figures would stay red like the clay.

ETCHING

Making an etching can be quite dangerous because chemicals are used. It is much safer to use a styrofoam press print sheet, which can make a very effective print.

WHAT YOU NEED
Pencil • Paper
Styrofoam sheet
Ballpoint pen • Ink
Paintbrush
Thick paper

PROJECT: TENNIS PRINT

Step 1. Make a drawing of a tennis game. Use simple shapes and lines. Copy it onto the styrofoam sheet.

Step 2. Use a ballpoint pen or blunt pencil to press into the drawing on the sheet to make lines. To make the shape of a tennis skirt or shorts, ask an adult to cut away these areas.

Step 3. Choose a colored ink and paint it onto the surface of the styrofoam. Press a thick piece of paper onto the ink and peel it off.

GALLERY

Le Jeu de Paume 1750
TENNIS ETCHING

COSTUME
Would you like to play tennis in these clothes? The clothing gives you a clue about the date of this tennis game.

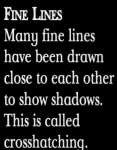

FINE LINES
Many fine lines have been drawn close to each other to show shadows. This is called crosshatching.

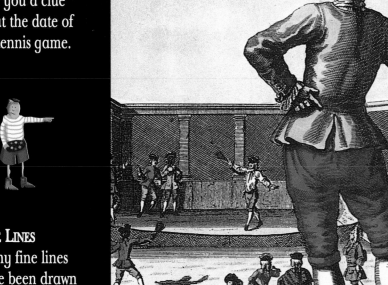

COLOR
Since this is a print, only a few colors have been used. Can you see what they are?

HISTORY
You can learn a great deal about the past by looking carefully at a work of art like this and comparing it with life today.

Illustrations for books were often made by etching. The artist would draw a detailed picture onto a sheet of metal and use acid to burn into the metal along the lines. Colors would then be put on the metal sheet. Sometimes the artist would add color or blacker lines after the print had been made.

DETAILED ICE SKATERS

Pieter Brueghel was one of a large family of painters. He often painted cool, wintery scenes with people enjoying the ice and snow. Look for some packaging materials that could make a collage of a snowy scene. Make sure they are cool colors.

GALLERY

Winter 1622-1635
PIETER BRUEGHEL (1564–1638)

DISTANCE
The people in the front (foreground) are much bigger than those people in the distance. Yet they are all carefully painted.

ACTIVITIES
How many different activities can you see going on? Did you spot a man who had fallen into the river?

In Holland during the winter, the canals and rivers used to freeze over, and people enjoyed skating on them. Pieter Brueghel painted many scenes of children and adults spending time together having fun.

PROJECT: SNOW AND ICE COLLAGE

Step 1. Ask an adult to help you to cut out a square from styrofoam packaging and draw mountains and a lake area on it in felt pen.

Step 2. Get an adult to help you cut away the styrofoam to make the mountains and lake shapes. Use a blunt knife very carefully. Paint the sky blue and add some of the cut out mountain shapes to make more mountains. Glue a piece of shiny paper for a pond.

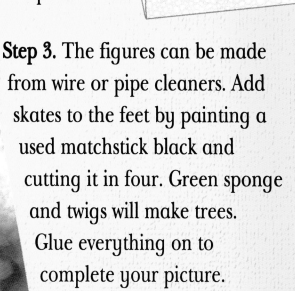

Step 3. The figures can be made from wire or pipe cleaners. Add skates to the feet by painting a used matchstick black and cutting it in four. Green sponge and twigs will make trees. Glue everything on to complete your picture.

3-D BALLET DANCERS

Degas made many paintings and sculptures of ballet dancers. This sculpture is full of life although it is made of metal. The same lively feeling can be given to a 3-D model made from cardboard.

WHAT YOU NEED
Thick cardboard
Pencil • Scissors
Paint • Paintbrush
Needle • Thread
Net

PROJECT: 3-D FIGURES

Step 1. Draw a figure on thick cardboard. You may need some help to cut it out. Degas chose a ballet dancer, but you can choose any sport.

Step 2. Paint both sides of your figure. If you chose a dancer, sew a line of stitches along the top of a small piece of net and tie it around the waist.

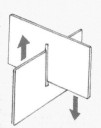

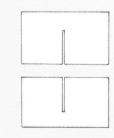

Step 3. To make a base, cut halfway through two pieces of cardboard and slot them together.

Step 4. Make a cut between your figure's feet. Slot your figure into the stand. You could make a whole troupe or a team.

18

GALLERY

Dancer 1896-1911
EDGAR DEGAS (1834–1917)

CLAY
First Degas made a ballet dancer from clay. It was then cast in bronze.

LIFELIKE
The final bronze dancer looks almost alive!

BRONZE
This ballet dancer is made from bronze, which is a metal. It starts as a liquid and is poured into a mold of the sculpture. When it is solid, it is polished until it shines.

Edgar Degas loved to go behind the scenes at the Paris theaters to watch the ballet dancers. He would take his sketchbook, pastels, pencils, and paints and make sketches. When he returned to his studio, he would turn his sketches into beautiful sculptures and paintings.

POINTILLIST CIRCUS

WHAT YOU NEED
Colored cardboard
Pencil • Scissors
Tracing paper
Felt-tip pens
Thread
Garden stick

The circus figures here look as though they could be attached to the top of the tent by wires. A group of circus figures hanging on threads would make a moving mobile that would look good hanging in your bedroom.

GALLERY

Le Cirque 1891
GEORGES SEURAT (1859–1891)

WHITE
The white horse and edge of the ring are the first things you look at.

CURVES
The curved line takes your eye around the painting and makes you feel as if you are in a circus ring.

COLORED DOTS
From a distance it is hard to see all the dots Seurat used, but if you look closely you can see each colored dot.

PROJECT: CIRCUS MOBILE

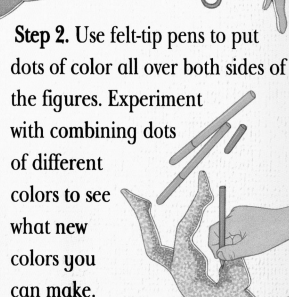

Step 1. Copy the circus figures from Seurat's painting onto colored cardboard. You can enlarge them on a photocopier and trace them. When your figures are finished, cut them out.

Georges Seurat trained as an artist in Paris. He tried different methods of painting, but is most famous for his style called "pointillism." You can see how he put dots of color next to each other in this picture of the circus. He spent a long time arranging different colored dots to see the effect they had, and the different colors they made, before he painted his pictures.

Step 2. Use felt-tip pens to put dots of color all over both sides of the figures. Experiment with combining dots of different colors to see what new colors you can make.

Step 3. Tie threads of different lengths onto each figure and then hang them from a garden stick. Add the long thread to the stick and hang it up in your room.

MINIATURE PAINTING

WHAT YOU NEED
White fabric
Cardboard • Pencil
Fabric paint
Ink • Glue
Thick paintbrush
Thin paintbrush
Sequins

Indian artists painted small pictures that usually told a story. They painted them on paper, wood, ivory, or fabric. Today, there are many different types of fabric paints and crayons that can be used to make a picture.

PROJECT: PAINTING FABRIC

Step 1. Find a small square of white fabric. Pin it to a piece of cardboard and sketch your picture with pencil. You could use the Moghul painting as a guide.

Step 2. Color your drawing by using fabric paint or ink. Color in the main areas first, using a thick brush.

Step 3. Use a fine brush for the details. Paint a frame around the edge and glue on sequins to decorate it when it is dry.

GALLERY

Prince with Falcon
MOGHUL STYLE (BEG. 17TH CENTURY)

SPORT
What sport do you think is illustrated here? The bird is a clue.

ILLUSTRATION
This painting could have been done to illustrate a book about life in the emperor's court.

COLOR
The man in the painting is a prince. He stands out in his brightly colored clothes.

MINIATURE
Paintings like this were often very small. Fine brushes of animal hair would be used to paint the delicate lines.

Long ago in northern India, artists painted pictures of everyday life at the emperor's court. Often these were miniatures, which means the paintings were very small. The artist would tell a story in paint about important events like elephants escaping or royal hunting expeditions.

ABSTRACT BALL PLAYER

Picasso used all sorts of weird and wonderful shapes in his paintings. He did not paint realistic pictures that showed exactly what things looked like. You can make a Picasso-style painting by finding shapes in scribbles!

GALLERY

Ball Players on the Beach 1928
PABLO PICASSO (1881–1973)

SHAPES
Look at the person drawn in black in the background. How is this one different in shape from the main person painted?

BODY
Look at the person playing with the ball. Can you figure out which bits are arms and legs?

PROJECT: FINDING SHAPES

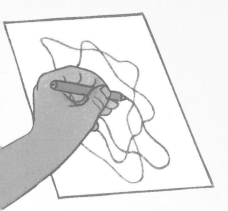

Step 1. Make some scribbles on a piece of paper using a fine pen. Take some time to look at the shapes you have made. Can you see shapes that could be made into figures or balls?

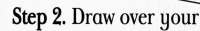

The Spanish artist Pablo Picasso changed how people saw art in the last century. He created paintings, sculptures, drawings, and ceramics that were all unusual or different from the work of other artists at that time. He used his imagination because he did not want his art to be realistic, like a photograph. When you look at one of his paintings, it may take you some time to figure out what some of the things in them are!

Step 2. Draw over your figure in a heavier pen. You could also color it in following the lines of the scribbles.

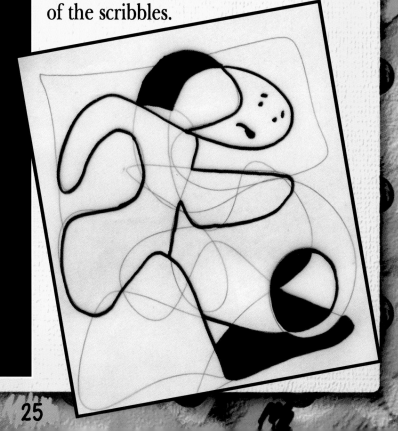

STREET SCENE IN OILS

Renoir used oil paints for this picture of his friends enjoying a day away from work. Pastels are also effective when drawing people. Why not try drawing some Parisian dancers, as Renoir has done, or some of your friends at a dance?

WHAT YOU NEED
Pastels
Sketchbook
Paper • Scissors
Used matchstick
Hairspray

PROJECT: **PASTEL DANCERS**

Step 1. Test your pastels in a sketchbook first to see how you can layer them or blend them. Draw a picture of people dancing. Fill in the background with different pastel shades.

Step 2. Color in the dancers. To get the effect of dappled light on the picture, scrape off some of the color with a used matchstick.

Step 3. Trim your picture and spray it with hairspray to prevent smudging.

GALLERY

The Ball at the Moulin de la Galette 1876
PIERRE AUGUSTE RENOIR (1841–1919)

COSTUME
Renoir has caught the spirit of the time by showing the details of the clothes. The hats and dresses show how Parisians dressed for a ball in 1876.

STREET LIFE
The people of Paris loved to spend their time outside in parks and squares. Here they are talking, eating, and dancing.

LIGHT
The light seems to be coming through the trees. Renoir has used a light-colored oil paint to show the effect of sunlight.

Many of Pierre Auguste Renoir's paintings show people enjoying themselves. He began work at the age of thirteen and spent his entire life painting the people and places he knew. The use of bright, fresh colors brought a cheerful touch to his work. He spent time with Monet painting outdoors and studying the effect of sunlight. During his lifetime Renoir became world famous. Today, people still travel all over the world to see his paintings.

PAINTED HORSE RIDERS

Many people enjoy riding along a beach like the figures in Gauguin's painting. They almost look as though they could jump out of the back of the picture. A 3-D effect can be achieved by cutting out horses and riders and adding them to a background.

PROJECT: 3-D HORSE RIDERS

Step 1. Paint a beach background on cardboard. Draw some horses and riders on another piece of cardboard. Paint them in warm colors. Use Gauguin's picture to help you choose shapes and colors.

Step 2. Cut out the horses and riders and glue a piece of folded cardboard onto the back of each.

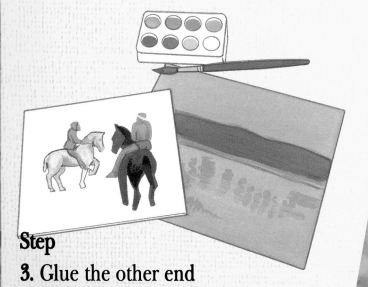

Step 3. Glue the other end of the folded cardboard to the background to finish the picture.

GALLERY

Riders on the Beach 1902
PAUL GAUGUIN (1848–1903)

TIME OF DAY
The warm but soft colors could be the early morning or evening light on the beach.

FREEDOM
The figures are not wearing many clothes and are riding their horses bareback.

BRUSH STROKES
Gauguin has used different kinds of brush strokes to blend colors together for the sky, sea, and sand.

FEELING
How does the painting make you feel? How do you think Gauguin felt when he painted it?

Paul Gauguin was born in Paris. However, he left his family and career in France to spend much of his life on the South Sea island of Tahiti. He hated city life and enjoyed living a simple life close to nature. Many of his paintings were of the tropical forests and beaches, where he loved the freedom of riding a horse. The warm colors he used show the enjoyment he had in his way of life.

SURREALIST SOCCER PLAYER

WHAT YOU NEED
Pencil • Scissors
Thick colored
cardboard
Tape • Thread
Paper fasteners

It is easy to turn a two-dimensional drawing into a movable figure if you use Salvador Dali's unusual soccer player to help you. Look closely at Dali's drawing, then draw the athlete of your choice and make a heart shape at the center.

GALLERY

Football Player c.1980
SALVADOR DALI (1904–1989)

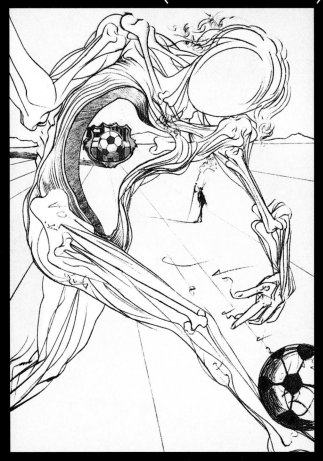

SKELETON
This soccer player has no skin or face, and is not at all like a real soccer player.

LAYERS
It is as if Dali has gotten under the skin of the soccer player to see his movements and feelings.

CENTER
What shape has been used to frame the ball at the center of the figure? What do you think it means?

DRAWING
You can see how skilled Dali was at drawing from the detailed skeleton.

PROJECT: MOVABLE FIGURE

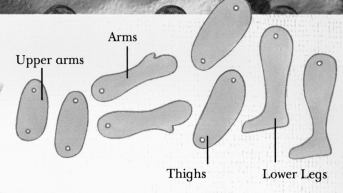

Upper arms · Arms · Thighs · Lower Legs

Step 1. Draw a head and body on thick colored cardboard. Cut out a heart shape from the chest. Tape the heart shape onto the side of the heart like a little door. Ask an adult to make holes as shown.

Step 2. Cut out two sets of arms and legs as shown above, and ask an adult to make holes as shown. Put your figure together using paper fasteners so that it moves.

After working in the United States for a number of years, Salvador Dali returned to Spain where he had been born. He was a member of the Surrealist movement of artists. His art was famous because he painted people, places, and objects in great detail, putting them together into a picture in an unusual way.

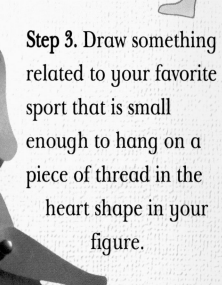

Step 3. Draw something related to your favorite sport that is small enough to hang on a piece of thread in the heart shape in your figure.

GLOSSARY

FOREGROUND The part of the view that is in the front of a picture.

MODEL A smaller than life three-dimensional sculpture of an animal, person, or object.

ABSTRACT Shapes and patterns grouped together to make a picture.

COLLAGE Placing different materials on a background to make a pattern or picture.

ETCHING Acid is used to cut out a picture into a piece of metal. Ink is then put on and a print made of it.

EXPRESSIONISM A style of art that uses color, line, and shape to show emotion rather than to make pictures that look like the real world.

POINTILLISM Dots of paint put close to each other which the eye turns into blocks of color.

REALISTIC A work of art that is made to look exactly like the real world.

SCULPTURE Making shapes from hard or soft materials, to make a person, animal, or design that can be looked at from all sides.

SURREALISM Art that brings together unusual objects and imaginary places that would not be seen in the real world.

THREE-DIMENSIONAL Sometimes shortened to 3-D. An object or work of art that you can walk all around and look at from all sides.

TONES The many different shades or tints of a color.

INDEX